THE RIVER CITY
HAGGADAH

אָשִׁירָה
לַיהוה

MOSESMUSES

NOTES

I wrote this Haggadah for celebrants who have no Hebrew, so everyone seated at our family's Passover can participate, question, and understand.

The book is a scaffolding to support and elevate the meal.

I think of the service as a musical ritual, even in English, and so followed my ear and my heart and the dictionary to summon the clearest language.

Nonetheless, every Seder is personal, and can take many forms: discussions of history, current events, individual recollections, jokes and fervent thanks.

Nobody really knows what the *Afikoman* (page 9) means— an internet search returns many explanations. In our house, it's hidden (set aside in the stage directions) and sought by the children to conclude the Seder. Usually accompanied by the words: "No dessert until…" Other families offer other rewards.

Some of the praise songs invite call and response:
"Enough/Dayenu" on pages 20-22, and
"Always returning" on pages 37-39
The Hallel, the Psalms of Praise (pages 35 -41), can be recited by the leader, or by volunteers. Our practice is to go around the table, and have each celebrant read a stanza.

The Hebrew on the front cover is from Exodus 15:1,
Moses' Song at the Red Sea.
It means, "I Sing to the Lord"

HIGH
LAND
BOOKS

ISBN: 978-1-7330907-5-9

THE JERUSALEM RIDER

In the Hebrew Bible, Israel is the name of Jacob's people,
it is not the name of the land promised to Abraham, the father
of many nations.

What is Jerusalem?

In Deuteronomy, Moses taught that, in the land across the
river, Israel will come "to the place the LORD your God shall
choose as a dwelling for his Name."

When Abraham bound Isaac on the Mount of Fear, and saw
the ram to sacrifice, he looked upon that dwelling place and
called it

"Adonai Yireh/יְהֹוָה ׀ יִרְאֶה/—the LORD sees."
That land was ruled by King Melchizedek, Noah's son Shem,
who called his city "Salem/שָׁלֵם/—Peace."

About that place, God reasoned: If I call my dwelling
"Yireh," Shem and the Semites will resent it.

If I call my city "Salem," Abraham will feel slighted. So I
will name my place "Jerusalem—He will see Peace."

Rabbi Berekiah added that, "while the place was still called
Salem, God made himself a tabernacle there and prayed,

'O that I may see the Temple building.'
And after Abraham sacrificed the ram in place of his son, God
saw the Temple built, destroyed, and built again."

According to the sages, Solomon's Temple was destroyed because
of three evils: idolatry, immorality, and bloodshed.

When that First Temple fell (on Tisha B'Av, the Ninth of
Av), prophecy ceased.

In the prophetic silence, some read history for signs.

The Second Temple fell on the same day, 716 years later,
even though people studied Torah, observed the 613
commandments, and practiced charity.

Why?

While the Second Temple stood, hatred without rightful
cause prevailed. Hatred without rightful cause is as grave as
idolatry, immorality, and bloodshed combined.

There is no Temple now.
There is a city called Jerusalem.
There is still hatred without rightful cause.
Who doesn't deem his hatred rightful?

The prophet Ezekiel's vision of a city called
    "Adonai Shammah/יְהוָה ׀ שָׁמָּה/—the LORD is There"
spells out in detail the plan of the Third Temple.
    And in that place, the School of Elijah explains, in those
days to come, the righteous will be given a new heart with an
impulse to good, not to evil.
    God will remove their stony heart, and replace it with a
heart of flesh.

My heart danced when they said, Go in:
I stood inside the doorway to Jerusalem:
Jerusalem, the city of the LORD of all

Creation, ruler of the law, of people
Speaking heart to heart, where dream, word, thought,
Justice, judgment, thanks, and praise

Agree, where meeting, people talk
About Jerusalem, and talking sing of peace,
        Their only greeting.

L.W.
Richmond, VA 2024/5784

SEARCH FOR LEAVEN

On the evening following the thirteenth of Nisan after evening service (if the first day of Passover falls on Sunday, on the evening following the twelfth of Nisan), the head of the household searches for leaven/ *chametz*—bread made with yeast—throughout the house. Customarily, a few pieces of bread are left about on purpose, so that the search for leaven is fruitful. Otherwise, the blessing before the ceremony would be pointless.

Before the ceremony of searching for leaven begins, light a candle and recite the following prayer:

Bless you, LORD our God, ruler of the universe,
Who gave us meaning, the commandments,
And taught us to remove the *chametz*.

Search for the leaven. Wrap any leaven that is found, and store it away until the next morning.
    After the leaven has been gathered and wrapped securely, say:

Any *chametz* that may still be in the house,
Which I have not seen or have not removed,
Is as if it does not exist, and is now like dust of the earth.

On the fourteenth of Nisan (if the first day of Passover falls on Sunday, on the thirteenth of Nisan), about ten o'clock in the morning, all the leaven remaining in the house along with all the bread collected during the search the night before is burned.
    At the burning of the leaven, recite:

Any *chametz* that may still be in the house,
Which I have or have not seen,
Which I have or have not removed,
Is as if it does not exist, and is now like dust of the earth.

PREPARE THE FOOD

When Passover falls on a Friday. so that it may be permissible to cook on that day for the Sabbath (which in this case is also *Yom Tov*, a festival, or good day), the head of the household must perform the ritual of *Eruv Tavshilin* before the festival.

Take some matzoh and some other food, such as fish or meat, put them on a plate, raise it, and recite:

Bless you, LORD our God, ruler of the universe,
Who gave us meaning, the commandments,
    and taught us about the *eruv*.
This *eruv* permits us to bake, cook,
    and to keep the food warm,
To light the candles, and to prepare all necessary things
    on the festival for the Sabbath.
This permission extends to us, and to all Jews living
    in this city.

SET THE TABLE

Before sunset, set three plates on the table. In one, put three matzohs; in the second, place a shank bone and a roasted egg, some horseradish (*maror*/bitter herbs), some celery or parsley sprigs (*karpas*), and the mixture of nuts, fruit and wine called *haroseth*; the third plate holds vinegar or brine.

ORDER OF THE PASSOVER SEDER

1. Kaddesh/ קַדֵּשׁ (reciting *Kiddush*, the blessing of the wine)
2. Urechatz/ וּרְחַץ (washing hands)
3. Karpas/ כַּרְפַּס (dipping greens in brine)
4. Yachatz/ יַחַץ (breaking the middle matzoh and hiding half—the *Afikoman*)
5. Maggid/ מַגִּיד (retelling the Passover story)
6. Rachatz/ רָחַץ (washing hands before the meal)
7. Motzi/ מוֹצִיא (blessing of bread)
8. Matza/ מַצָּה (blessing the matzoh)
9. Maror/ מָרוֹר (eating the bitter herb)
10. Korech/ כֹּרֵךְ (eating the bitter herb and matzoh together)
11. Shulchan Orech/ שֻׁלְחָן עֹרֵךְ (serving the Festival meal)
12. Tzafoon/ צָפוּן (sharing the *Afikoman*)
13. Barech/ בָּרֵךְ (saying grace after the meal)
14. Hallel/ הַלֵּל (reciting the songs of praise)
15. Nirtzah/ נִרְצָה (concluding the Seder)

On a Friday night, Sabbath eve, begin the Seder here.

At eighteen minutes before sunset, light two Shabbat candles—
each candle is a signal, one "to remember" and one "to do"—
and recite the this blessing:

Bless you, maker of the universe
Who has given us the law, and taught us
To light the Sabbath lamps.

Barukh attah adonai eloheinu melech ha'olam
asher kidshanu b'mitzvotav,
v'tzivanu l'hadliq ner shel shabbat

בָּרוּךְ אַתָּה יְיָ אֱלֹהֵיתוּ מֶלֶךְ הָעוֹלָם
אֲשֶׁר קִדְּשָׁנוּ בְּמִצְוֹתָיו
וְצִוָּנוּ לְהַדְלִיק נֵר שֶׁל שַׁבָּת

KADDESH/קַדֵּשׁ

On a weekday, the seder begins here.

Fill the first cup of wine, hold it in your right hand, and
recite this blessing:

Bless you, LORD our God, ruler of the universe,
who created the fruit of the vine.

Barukh attah adonai eloheinu melech ha'olam
boré p'ri ha'gafen

בָּרוּךְ אַתָּה ה' אֱלֹהֵינוּ מֶלֶךְ הָעוֹלָם
בּוֹרֵא פְּרִי הַגָּפֶן

Bless you, LORD our God, ruler of the universe,
who chose us from the throng of people
and singled us out among nations
by giving us the commandments,
knowledge of life and good.
You gave festivals for happy times,
and appointed holidays and seasons for rejoicing.
Such is this Day of the Feast of Unleavened Bread,
when we gather to remember our going out
from Egypt, and to taste our freedom.
For you chose us among all others to keep
and celebrate your festivals
with joy and fervor, the marks of your love and favor.

Bless you, God of Israel, who makes holy festivals.

Barukh attah adonai mi qadddesh
v' yisrael v' ha-zmanim

בָּרוּךְ אַתָּה יְיָ מְקַדֵּשׁ
וְ יִשְׂרָאֵל וְהַזְּמַנִּים

8

Bless you, LORD our God, ruler of the universe,
who has kept us living
and let us celebrate this happy season.

Barukh attah adonai eloheinu melech ha'olam
shehechianu v'kimanu v'higianu lazman hazzeh

בָּרוּךְ אַתָּה ה' אֱלֹהֵינוּ מֶלֶךְ הָעוֹלָם
שֶׁהֶחֱיָנוּ וְקִיְּמָנוּ וְהִגִּיעָנוּ לַזְּמַן הַזֶּה

Drink the first cup of wine.

URECHATZ/ וּרְחַץ

Wash hands, without reciting a blessing.

KARPAS/ כַּרְפַּס

The leader of the Seder dips greens in brine or vinegar, and distributes
them in pieces around the table.
All recite the following blessing, then eat the Karpas.

Bless you, LORD our God, ruler of the universe,
who makes the earth fruitful.

Barukh attah adonai eloheinu melech ha'olam
boré p'ri ha'adamah

בָּרוּךְ אַתָּה ה' אֱלֹהֵינוּ מֶלֶךְ הָעוֹלָם
בּוֹרֵא פְּרִי הָאֲדָמָה

YACHATZ/ יַחַץ

The leader breaks the middle matzoh in half, leaving one part between
the two whole matzohs and sets aside the other half as the Afikoman.

9

MAGGID/ מַגִּיד

Fill the second cup of wine.
The leader uncovers the matzohs and, raising the plate for all to see,
     says:

This is the bread of affliction,
     which our parents ate in Egypt.
Let all the hungry come and eat.
Let all the needy come and celebrate the Passover.
Now we are here; next year may we be
     in the Land of Promise.
Now we are slaves; next year may we be free.

The leader puts down the plate, and covers the matzoh.

The youngest person present asks the four questions:

What makes this night different from all other nights?
1. On any other night we eat both leavened and
unleavened bread.
     This night, why do we eat only unleavened bread?
2. On any other night we eat leafy greens of all kinds.
     This night, why do we eat only bitter herbs?
3. On any other night we do not dip our herbs even once.
     This night, why do we dip them twice?
4. On any other night we eat our meals either sitting
upright, or leaning over.
     This night, why do we all lean?

The leader uncovers the matzoh, and answers:

When we were Pharaoh's slaves in Egypt, the LORD our
God brought us out from there
     with a mighty hand and an outstretched arm.
Now, if God had not brought our ancestors out

from Egypt, then all of us—our children and our
children's children—might still be slaves in Egypt.
So, even if we all were wise, all old, all steady, all
learned in the ways of God, we should still retell
the story of the going out from Egypt.
And the more one speaks about the Exodus,
the more one should be praised.

Long ago, Rabbi Eliezer, Rabbi Joshua, Rabbi Eleazar
ben Azariah and Rabbi Tarfon met in the town of Bene
Barak and sat up all night talking about the departure
from Egypt. At sunrise, their students called to them:
"Masters, it is time to recite the morning Sh'ma,"
and they prayed:

Hear, O Israel, the LORD our God, the LORD is One[a]

Sh'ma Israel, adonai eloheinu, adonai eḥad

שמע ישראל יהוה אלהינו יהוה אחד

Eleazar son of Azariah said: "I have lived to be seventy
years old, but I never understood why the story of the
Exodus should be told at night until Ben Zoma explained
what Moses wrote in Deuteronomy,
'So that you may remember the day when you
came out of the land of Egypt all the days of your life.'
'The days of your life' would mean the days only, but
'all the days of your life' includes the nights as well."

The sages of Israel go further: "'The days of your life'
refers to this world, while 'All the days of your life'
includes the time to come.'"

---

a. Deuteronomy 6:4

Bless the One, Blessed be He,
who gave the Torah to his people Israel.
Bless the LORD.

Barukh ha'maqom, barukh hu
barukh shenatan torah l'amo israel
barukh hu

בָּרוּךְ הַמָּקוֹם בָּרוּךְ הוּא
בָּרוּךְ שֶׁנָּתַן תּוֹרָה לְעַמּוֹ יִשְׂרָאֵל
בָּרוּךְ הוּא

The Torah speaks of four kinds of children:
The wise child, the wicked, the simple one,
    the one too young to know to ask.
The wise child asks:
    "What do they mean, these testimonies, and statutes,
    and judgments, which the One our God
    has commanded us in the books of Moses?"
To that child, explain all the laws of Passover,
    down to the very last detail about the Afikoman.
The wicked child asks:
    "What do you mean by this service?"
    By saying "you," and not "we" or "me," he excludes
    himself from the group, and denies God.
Answer that child bluntly:
    Had you been there in Egypt,
    you would not have been redeemed.
The simple child asks:
    "What is this?"
Answer, "With a strong hand, God brought us out
    from Egypt, from the house of bondage."
And the child too young to ask?
    It is written: "Teach your children in that day, saying,
    'This is done because of that which the LORD
    did for me when I came forth out of Egypt.'"

Once people only worshipped self-made idols,
　　but now we know about the One,
　　the maker of the universe,
and worship in the way recorded in the Torah:

"Joshua said to all the people:
　　The LORD God of Israel tells us that, in the old days,
our ancestors lived the across the Euphrates—Abraham's
father Terah, and Nachor —and they served other gods.

　　I took your father Abraham from there, and led him
throughout the land of Canaan, and multiplied his seed,
and gave him Isaac.

　　And I gave Isaac two sons, Jacob and Esau.
I gave Esau Mount Seir east of Canaan as a homeland.
But Jacob and his children went down into Egypt."

　　　　Bless the One, who kept the promise to Israel.
　　　　　　　　Blessed He.

　　　Barukh shomer ha'v'tachato l'israel barukh hu

בָּרוּךְ שׁוֹמֵר הַבְטָחָתוֹ לְיִשְׂרָאֵל בָּרוּךְ הוּא

From the beginning of time, the One saw the end of our
bondage, and told old, childless Abram (who became
Abraham) about it in a vision:

　　"And he said: Know for certain that your children
will be strangers in a land that is not theirs.

　　And that nation will enslave them and oppress them
four hundred years;
　　know too I will judge that slavemaster nation;
　　and they will come out, free and rich."

Raise the cup of wine and say:

This promise, which God made to Abraham and his
children, God also made to us, in every generation.

More than once, in every generation, people rise up
against us to destroy us, but the One we praise delivers us
from the destroyers' hands.

Listen to what Jacob's uncle Laban the Aramaean tried to
do against him.
 Pharaoh condemned only the male children, but
Laban tried to take Jacob's whole family away from him.
 It is written in Deuteronomy:
"My father fled Laban, ready to perish. He went down
into Egypt, few in number, and sojourned there
and became a nation, great, mighty, and populous."

"He went down into Egypt,"
 in obedience to God's word,

"and sojourned there."
 Genesis records that Jacob (Israel) did not mean to
settle in Egypt.
 Jacob's sons told Pharaoh, "We come to stay a while
in the land. Your servants have no pasture for their flocks
because the famine is great in Canaan. For now, let us
dwell in the land of Goshen."

"Few in number," as it is written:
 "Your fathers went down into Egypt with seventy
persons; and now the LORD your God has made you
many as the stars of heaven."

"And there they became a nation,"
 which teaches us that they could be told apart from
the Egyptians.

"Great and mighty," as described in Exodus:
"And the children of Israel were fruitful, and
increased abundantly, and multiplied, and waxed mighty;
and the land was filled with them."

"And populous," as Ezekiel witnessed:
"I have caused you to multiply
like sprouts in the field, and you have increased
and grown great."

"And the Egyptians grew harsh, and oppressed us, and
made us slave labor."

"The Egyptians grew harsh," the story goes, and said:
"Come, let us plan shrewdly, in case their numbers
increase and, should war break out, they join
our enemies and fight against us,
and get themselves out of the land."

"And oppressed us," as it is told:
"Therefore they set slave drivers over them
to afflict them with their burdens. And they built
treasure cities for Pharaoh, Pithom and Raamses."

"And made us slave labor," as it is said:
"And the Egyptians made the children of Israel
serve, mercilessly."

"And we cried to the LORD, God of our fathers, and
the LORD heard our voice, and looked on our slavery,
and our misery, and our oppression."

"And we cried to the LORD God of our fathers," as is
recorded:

"Time passed, and the king of Egypt died.
The children of Israel groaned in bondage, and
cried out, and their cry of distress rose up to God."

"The LORD heard our voice," as it is said:
"And God heard their groaning, and God
remembered his covenant with Abraham,
with Isaac, and with Jacob."

"And looked on our slavery," meaning
husbands and wives slept apart, so they would
not bear children for Pharaoh to abuse, as it is told:
"And God looked upon the children of Israel,
and God respected them."

"And our misery,"—the drowning of the male children—
as it is written:
"And Pharaoh charged all his people, saying,
Every son that is born you shall cast into the river,
and every daughter you shall save alive."

"And our oppression," as it is recorded:
"Now therefore, behold: the cry of the children
of Israel is come to me: and I have also seen
how the Egyptians oppress them."

"And the LORD brought us forth out of Egypt with a
mighty hand, and with an outstretched arm, and with great
terribleness, and with signs, and with wonders."

"And the LORD brought us forth out of Egypt,"
not by the hand of an angel, not by the hand
of a seraph, not by the hand of a messenger,

but the Holy One, Blessed be He, himself
brought us out, as is said:

"For I will pass through the land of Egypt this night,
and will smite all the firstborn in the land of Egypt,
both man and beast; and against all the gods of Egypt
I will execute judgment: I am the LORD."

"For I will pass through the land of Egypt this night:"
    I, and not an angel.

"And will smite all the firstborn in the land of Egypt:"
    I, and not a seraph.

"And against all the gods of Egypt I will execute
judgment:"
    I, and not a messenger.

"I am the LORD:"
    I am that I am and no other.

"With a mighty hand,"—sickness—as it is told:
    "Behold, the hand of the LORD is upon your cattle
    which is in the field, upon the horses, upon the asses,
    upon the camels, upon the oxen, and upon the sheep:
    there shall be a truly grievous murrain."

"And with an outstretched arm,"—the sword—as is
written in Chronicles:
    "A drawn sword in his hand stretched out
    over Jerusalem."

"And with great terribleness,"—the Divine Presence
revealed—as Moses said in Deuteronomy:

"Has God tried to go and take a nation from
the midst of another nation, by temptations, by signs,
and by wonders, and by war, and by a mighty hand,
and by a stretched out arm, and by great terrors,
all those things the LORD your God did for you
in Egypt before your own eyes?"

"And with signs,"—the rod of Moses—as has been told:
"And you shall take this rod in your hand; with it
you shall do signs."

"And with wonders,"—the river Nile water turned to
blood—as God declared in the prophet Joel:
"And I will show wonders in the heavens
and in the earth:

Spill a drop of wine for each of these three:

Blood,
and Fire,
and Pillars of Smoke."

Other teachers say:
"With a mighty hand" stands for two plagues;
"and with an outstretched arm"—stands for two;
"and with great terribleness"—two;
"and with signs"—two;
"and with wonders"—two.

These make the ten plagues which the Holy One brought
upon the Egyptians in Egypt:

Spill one drop of wine for each of the ten plagues

Blood	Dam/דָּם
Frogs	Tzfardea/צְפַרְדֵּעַ
Lice	Kinim/כִּנִּים
Beasts	Arov/עָרוֹב
Pestilence	Dever/דֶּבֶר
Boils	Shchin/שְׁחִין
Hail	Barad/בָּרָד
Locusts	Arbeh/אַרְבֶּה
Darkness	Ḥoshech/חֹשֶׁךְ
Slaying of the First-born	Makat Bechoroth/ מַכַּת בְּכוֹרוֹת

Rabbi Judah recalled the plagues with this mnemonic:

Spill three drops of wine, one for each watchword

DeTZaKh/דְּצַ"ךְ   ADaSH/עַדַ"שׁ   BeACHaB/בְּאַחַ"ב.

Rabbi Jose the Galilean asked:

How do we know that the Egyptians were smitten with ten plagues in Egypt, and with fifty plagues by the Red Sea?

He answered that, with regards to Egypt, it is written: "Then the magicians said to Pharaoh, 'This is the finger of God,' and Pharaoh's heart was hardened, and he did not listen to them, just as the LORD said."

With respect to the Red Sea, it is written: "When Israel saw what the great hand of the LORD did to the Egyptians, the people feared the LORD, and believed the LORD and his servant Moses."

See?

One finger for each plague in Egypt: ten plagues.

But at the Red Sea, the whole hand of God,

five fingers ten times: fifty plagues.

Rabbi Eliezer countered:

Every plague God visited upon the Egyptians had the force of four plagues.

Psalm 78 recounts:
"He cast upon them the fierceness of his anger, wrath, and indignation, and trouble, by sending evil angels among them."

"Wrath" makes one; "indignation", two;

"trouble" three; "evil angels", four.

Therefore, the Egyptians were smitten with forty plagues in Egypt, and with two hundred plagues by the Red Sea shore.

Rabbi Akiva asked:

Where do we learn that each and every plague the Holy One visited upon the Egyptians was equal to five plagues?

The same psalm says:
"The fierceness of his anger", one; "wrath", two; "indignation" three; "trouble" four; "sending evil angels" makes five times.

Thus, we have ten times five: fifty plagues in Egypt; and five times fifty: two hundred fifty plagues at the Red Sea.

How many blessings God has given Israel.
Had God brought us out from Egypt
     And not visited them with judgment
It would have been   Enough

                            Dayenu/ דַּיֵּנוּ

Had God visited them with judgment
     And not cast down their idols

                            Dayenu/ דַּיֵּנוּ

Enough

Had God destroyed their idols
    And not slain their firstborn

                Dayenu/ דַּיֵּנוּ
                Enough

Had God only slain their firstborn
    And not given us their substance

                Dayenu/ דַּיֵּנוּ
                Enough

Had God just given us their substance
    And not parted the Red Sea for us

                Dayenu/ דַּיֵּנוּ
                Enough

Had God parted the Red Sea for us
    And not let us walk upon the dry sea bed

                Dayenu/ דַּיֵּנוּ
                Enough

Had God led us across the dry sea bed
    And not drowned our pursuers in its waters

                Dayenu/ דַּיֵּנוּ
                Enough

Had God drowned our pursuers in its waters
    And not kept us forty years in the wilderness

                Dayenu/דַּיֵּנוּ
                Enough

Had God but kept us forty years in the wilderness
    And not fed us with manna

                Dayenu/ דַּיֵּנוּ
                Enough

Had God just fed us with manna
    And not given us the Sabbath rest

                Dayenu/ דַּיֵּנוּ
                Enough

Had God given us the Sabbath rest

And not led us to the foot of Sinai

Dayenu/ דַּיֵּנוּ

Enough

Had God brought us to the foot of Sinai
And not taught us the Torah

Dayenu/ דַּיֵּנוּ

Enough

Had God taught us the Torah
And not brought us into the Land

Dayenu/ דַּיֵּנוּ

Enough

Had God brought us into the Land
And not built the Temple there
It would have been   Enough

Dayenu/ דַּיֵּנוּ

God has showered blessings on us,

More than we can count:

God brought us out of Egypt,

And judged the Egyptians,

Cast down their idols,

And slew their firstborn,

Gave us their riches,

And parted the seas for us,

Let us walk the dry sea bed,

And drowned our pursuers,

Kept us alive forty years in the wilderness,

And fed us with manna,

Gave us the Sabbath,

And led us to Mount Sinai,

And there taught us Torah,

And brought us into the Land,

And there built the Temple

Where we might atone for our sins.

Rabbi Gamaliel used to say,

"Whoever fails to mention these three things on Passover has not satisfied his obligation: The Passover offering, the unleavened bread, the bitter herbs."

Why did our parents eat the Passover lamb when the Temple still stood in Jerusalem?

Because God passed over our parents' houses in Egypt, and we, too, say what is written:

"This is the sacrifice of the LORD's Passover, who passed over the houses of the children of Israel in Egypt, when he smote the Egyptians, and delivered our houses.

And the people bowed heads, and worshipped."

The leader lifts up the matzoh and shows it to the celebrants:

This matzoh, why do we eat it?

Because the dough had not yet risen when the King of All, the holy Name, revealed himself to our parents in Egypt, and redeemed them. So it is told:

"They baked unleavened cakes with the dough they brought forth out of Egypt. It was not leavened, because they were thrust out of Egypt, and could not wait for the dough to rise, and had not prepared any food for themselves."

The Seder leader lifts up the bitter herbs and shows it to the celebrants:

These bitter herbs, why do we eat them?

Because the Egyptians embittered the lives of our ancestors. It is recorded:

> "They made their lives bitter with hard bondage,
> toting mortar and brick, forced to do all kinds of work
> in the field: all their service was merciless."

The leader of the Seder covers the matzoh, and continues:

In every generation, every person must learn and
understand how "I, personally, have come forth out of
Egypt." So we are instructed:
> "You shall show your child in that day, saying,
> 'We keep the Passover in this way to remember
> what the LORD did for me when I came forth
> out of Egypt.'"

The Holy One redeemed not only our forebears, but our
selves as well, all at once, over time. As it is written:
> "The LORD brought us out from there, that he might
> bring us in, to give us the land which he promised
> to our parents."

Everyone, lift up your wine cups and say:

Therefore we say our thanks in prayer
and song and thought and deed and blessing.
Look at all the wonders made for all
> who came before, and for us:
> for us—the slaves made free; for us
> the crying stopped, and mourning took a holiday;
> for us—the light from darkness. Let us
> say a new song, naming being praise.

Replace the wine cups on the table. One person recites:

The work is never done.
Sunset, sunrise, sky
A high chair spilling
Light crumbs on the floor.
As before, we sweep them
Into heaps, find families
Where once the barren
Wasted time like water
And a mother bears.

[Psalm 113]

When Israel went up from Egypt,
A house in a house of no law with strange language,
    The land filled its promise to Jacob.
The sea saw the children on foot and drew back.
    Jordan turned aside.
Boulders skipped down mountainsides like rams
    Jump, like spring lambs.
        What quailed the sea so it fled?
        What shunted Jordan?
    Skipped the mountainside?
The presence, God, which makes land pitch
    Made rock melt into standing pools,
        Cliffs spout fountains.

[Psalm 114]

All raise their cup of wine and say:

Bless you LORD our God, Maker of the Universe,
    who redeemed our mothers and fathers from Egypt,
    and have brought us to this night
    when we eat unleavened bread and bitter herbs.

Thus may you, LORD our God, God of the Hebrews,
    bring us to future times and festivals in peace.
Bring us to God's city, to rebuild Jerusalem,
    where we may serve you and celebrate anew
    the acceptable offering.
Then we will sing you a new song of thanks
    for the deliverance of our people, and our souls.

Bless you, LORD our God, who delivers your people.

Bless you, LORD our God, ruler of the universe,
who created the fruit of the vine.

Barukh attah adonai eloheinu melech ha'olam
boré p'ri ha'gafen

בָּרוּךְ אַתָּה ה' אֱלֹהֵינוּ מֶלֶךְ הָעוֹלָם בּוֹרֵא פְּרִי הַגָּפֶן

Drink the second cup of wine while leaning to the left.

RACHZA/ רַחַץ

All wash hands, and say:

Bless you, LORD our God, ruler of the universe,
who made us holy with your commandments,
and told us to wash our hands.

Barukh attah adonai eloheinu melech ha'olam
asher kidshanu bemitzvotav
ve-tzivanu al netilat yadayim.

בָּרוּךְ אַתָּה ה' אֱלֹהֵינוּ מֶלֶךְ הָעוֹלָם
אֲשֶׁר קִדְּשָׁנוּ בְּמִצְוֹתָיו וְצִוָּנוּ עַל נְטִילַת יָדַיִם

MOTZI /מוֹצִיא

Holding all three matzot, the leader of the Seder says:

Bless you, LORD our God, ruler of the universe,
who brings forth bread from the earth.

Barukh attah adonai eloheinu melech ha'olam
ha'motzi lechem min ha'aretz.

בָּרוּךְ אַתָּה ה' אֱלֹהֵינוּ מֶלֶךְ הָעוֹלָם
הַמּוֹצִיא לֶחֶם מִן הָאָרֶץ

MATZA /מַצָּה

The Seder leader breaks pieces from the upper and middle matzoh,
and distributes them around the table.

Holding only the top and broken middle matzoh, the leader says:

Bless you, LORD our God, ruler of the universe,
who made us holy with your commandments, and told us
to eat unleavened bread.

Barukh attah adonai eloheinu melech ha'olam
asher kidshanu bemitzvotav ve'tzivanu al achilat matza.

בָּרוּךְ אַתָּה ה' אֱלֹהֵינוּ מֶלֶךְ הָעוֹלָם
אֲשֶׁר קִדְּשָׁנוּ בְּמִצְוֹתָיו וְצִוָּנוּ עַל אֲכִילַת מַצָּה

Eat the matzoh.

MAROR/ מָרוֹר

The leader of the Seder dips the bitter herbs in haroseth, and says:

Bless you, LORD our God, ruler of the universe,
who made us holy with your commandments, and told us
to eat the bitter herb.

Barukh attah adonai eloheinu melech ha'olam
asher kidshanu bemitzvotav ve'tzivanu al achilat maror.

בָּרוּךְ אַתָּה ה' אֱלֹהֵינוּ מֶלֶךְ הָעוֹלָם
אֲשֶׁר קִדְּשָׁנוּ בְּמִצְוֹתָיו וְצִוָּנוּ עַל אֲכִילַת מָרוֹר

Share out and eat the bitter herb.

KORECH/ כֹּרֵךְ

The leader of the Seder makes a sandwich of bitter herbs between two
pieces of the bottom matzoh.
Before eating it, he says:

In Rabbi Hillel's time, when the Temple still stood in
Jerusalem, that sage would put the bitter herb between the
matzoh, and eat them together, to fulfill the words of the
Book of Numbers: "They shall…eat it with
                    unleavened bread and bitter herbs."

SHULCHAN ORECH/ שֻׁלְחָן עֹרֵךְ

Remove the Seder plate, and eat the Passover meal.
The first course is often a hard-cooked egg.
After eating the meal, return the Seder plate to the table.

TZAFOON/ צָפוּן

Share out the matzoh which has been set aside for the Afikoman among the company.

BARECH/ בָּרֵךְ

All recite:

When we returned from far away
Our home looked as it looks in dreams:
The sun shines, gates swing
Open of themselves, and someone
Sings a song we had forgotten
As we now remember laughter.
Then strangers said, Great things
Were done for them.

> The LORD

Did great things for us then. A good.
But you must do great things again,
Because we live with heaviness
And twist and scatter like a river
Delta bogged in marsh and reeds.
We started sadly so we'd end up
Smiling, for anyone begins, sows
Seed with tears to reap his own,
The happy harvest, no?

> [Psalm 126]

Fill the third cup of wine.
The leader of the Seder says:

Let us say Grace.

The adults respond:

May the Name of the LORD be blessed now and ever.

The leader of the Seder says:

Let us bless the One whose food we have eaten.

The adults respond:

Let us bless the One whose food we have eaten
and through whose goodness we live.

The leader says:

Bless the LORD, blessed the Name.

All respond:

Bless you, LORD our God, maker of the universe,
who feeds the world from goodness, feeds all that lives
    with purpose and feeling, with bread for being,
    with food for all the creatures he has made,
    and makes, and kept, and touched, and fed
    and has, and will, forever.

Thank you for the place, the land you gave
    to those who went before us, and to us.
Thanks for bringing us up from Egypt, out of slavery,
    and teaching us to sign the contract with our bodies,
    for giving us your book, the wisdom and the law
    by which we know life and good from death and evil.

For these gifts, and for our food which never fails us,
we thank you, and we bless your name as Moses wrote:
    "When you have eaten and are full,
    then you shall bless the LORD your God
    for the good land which he has given you."
Bless you, o LORD, for the land and for the food.

Remember kindly, LORD our God, Israel,
    your chosen people and Jerusalem, your city.
Look on Zion, mount of glory, and the kingdom
    of the House of David, your anointed
and regard the Temple, where your holy name is called.

And hear us, father, lead us, guard us, keep us, teach us,
        carry us away from all our troubles, God,
            and quickly, in our day,
so we do not need the gifts or loans
        that flesh and blood extend us.
But only let us take the needful, God,
        from your hand only, always open, full,
            without shame or disgrace.

Our God—our fathers' mothers' fathers' God—
        hear and remember us, our offspring
and Jerusalem, the messiah
        son of David and all Israel—
Let all return to you, and you
        return us to ourselves.
And may we all be saved
        by our remembering
this Festival of the Unleavened Bread.

Remember us, o God, for good.
We look to you, and may we live
to see you build Jerusalem, and quickly.
Bless you, LORD, the builder of Jerusalem.

        Amen.

Bless you, LORD our God, master of the universe,
    father, leader, ruler, maker, teacher,
God of Jacob, shepherd of Israel,
    king and doer of the good,
of favor, feeling, knowing, teaching
    kindness, grace and ease—
From the side of mercy
    save us as you have and will.

Out of mercy— may God always rule.
Out of mercy— bless the heavens and the earth.
Out of mercy— praise the maker.
Out of mercy— may the LORD sustain us.
Out of mercy— may our yoke be broken and the people
    led into the land.
Out of mercy— may God bless this house and table
    where unleavened bread was broken.
Out of mercy— may God send Elijah
    (ever remembered for good)
    to us, to bring us news of comfort and redemption.
Out of mercy— may God bless us here assembled,
    and all that is ours, even as our fathers Abraham,
    Isaac and Jacob were blessed with the blessing,
        and let us say, Amen.

Out of mercy— may God grant us a day of rest
    after this life.
Out of mercy— let that day be altogether good.
Out of mercy— let us live to see the world to come,
    the promise made to David and his seed fulfilled,
    the peace and music of the stars be known in Israel,
        and let us say, Amen.

"He is the tower of salvation for his king,
      And shows mercy to his chosen:
To David, and to his seed for evermore."
The maker of peace in high places
Shall make peace for us, and all Israel,
            So say, Amen.

O fear the LORD, you who hear and do:
      Nothing wants for those who fear him.
Young lions lack, and suffer hunger:
      but those who seek the One shall not want
      any good thing.
O give thanks to the LORD; for he is good:
      his mercy lasts for ever.
You open your hand,
      and answer the desire of every living thing.
Blessed is the one who trusts in the One,
      and whose hope is the LORD's.
I have been young, and now am old,
yet I have not seen the upright soul forsaken,
      nor his seed begging bread.
The Name gives strength to his people;
The LORD will bless his people with peace.

Lift your cups of wine and say:

Bless you, LORD our God, ruler of the universe,
      who created the fruit of the vine.

Barukh attah adonai eloheinu melech ha'olam
            boré p'ri ha'gafen.

בָּרוּךְ אַתָּה ה' אֱלֹהֵינוּ מֶלֶךְ הָעוֹלָם
בּוֹרֵא פְּרִי הַגָּפֶן

Drink the third cup of wine while reclining.

One celebrant rises from the table and, opening the door, recites the following verses:

Pour out your wrath upon the peoples
   that have not known you,
and upon the nations
   that have not called upon your name.
For they have devoured Jacob,
   and laid waste his dwellingplace.
Pour out your indignation upon them,
   and let your wrathful anger take hold of them.
Persecute and destroy them in anger
   from under the heavens of the LORD.

Close the door, and return to the table
Fill the fourth cup, and finish reciting:

HALLEL/ הַלֵּל

[Psalms 115-118; 136]

Not for our sake, but so strangers will not say
    Where is god?
In the sky? does he listen? then polish
    Their bumpers and crystal,
And go right on braying, and looking not seeing:
    These hummers with tin ears, they
Wrinkle their noses, grope hard under covers,
    And stumble, and cry out:
They are what they worship, and fashion, and trust.

    Admit what you can't know,
    And can't see, and grow up
To fear it. Grow rich and old, less
Than the maker of earth and sky,
    Gifts to the living. Give
Life. For what good do the dead do?
    Can they worship, sing praises?
    For as long as you can, live
    And praise, live and praise.

For once when I cried out somebody listened:
The LORD took my complaint for a song
Belted at the top of my lungs
In a shower of troubles, good
Even if off key. Surrounded by death
Loving liars, by fires banked inside
My nature, I stumbled over simple things:
A shoe untied, the pillow never smooth,
A night cough, hum of strangers' tires.

The gift has been given. So, low but alive,
I said what I believed: that greed succeeds
Where grace can not, that one idea can kill
A world of simple pleasures, cup and spoon.
Stir them. Don't speak quickly, savor
The hot cider, candied ginger on the tongue,
Heavy cloud shrugged off my shoulders.
I promise to be more than one of those
(What, still alive? He lived? He died?) who never
Show their heart or read the lips of mumblers
In the public record: I call upon the LORD,
Am called upon, to praise in easy words:
A truth should come out plain and make good sense,
So truth will find a friendly audience.

LORD,
All living
Utter praises:
Dead ones don't.
      Or:
Heaven covers
Yesterday with
Morning, always:
Now praise.

Thank goodness just one god always returning.
Let children learn to say, "Always returning."
Let those who lead thought say, "Always returning."
Let those who've seen fear say, "Always returning."

      I called from my narrow self:
      The great expanse answered,
Said: If God is for you, what matter

Who hates you. Far better to trust
    Found disorder than tugs
    Of war, others: give up
    To the sky, not mean men.

    Surrounded, I cut off
Their shouts in mid-sentence, shaved
Fringes off whatever small point
They boasted: bee swarms and smoke
    Crackling fired thorns, pinky rings,
Philistine foreskins heaped up on the floor.

    A hip-slapper.
Winners' tents pitch, but the fortunate
Dancer chose pebbles, more killing
Than coping stones dropped from a temple wall.
    Shelter's how things fall out;
    Hope is tomorrow's door.

Happy for good from the name I can't say aloud,
Blue hazes wind through the horns of the altar.
Praise for the ornament, heart plays the instrument:
Thank goodness just one god always returning.
Thank the LORD, there is good in life

                    Always returning
Thank the LORD there is just one god

                    Always returning
Thank the LORD there are many ways

                    Always returning
One who makes wondering

                    Always returning
One who knows sky as mind

                    Always returning

Set gem land in ocean rings

                                        Always returning

Who mounted the living lights

                                        Always returning

The sun to show daytime

                                        Always returning

Moon and stars steering nights

                                        Always returning

Who smote Egypt's firstborn

                                        Always returning

Led Israel's children out

                                        Always returning

Played strong hand at arms' length

                                        Always returning

Who parted the Red Sea reeds

                                        Always returning

A causeway for Israel

                                        Always returning

But swallowed up following Pharaoh and chariots

                                        Always returning

Whose pillar led people through desert waste

                                        Always returning

Who toppled old kingdoms

                                        Always returning

Who killed famous rulers,

                                        Always returning

Crushed Sihon of Heshbon,

                                        Always returning

Erased Og of Bashan,

                                        Always returning

Gave their lands to our fathers,

                                        Always returning

His children of Israel

                                        Always returning

Who remembered us, sunken hulks

                                    Always returning

And floated us, salvaged and

                                    Always returning

Who finds food for all living things

                                    Always returning

Thank the LORD there is one God, good

                                    Always returning

All that lives, by breathing
    makes a blessing of your name,
LORD, and the spirit makes its praise when it remembers
How it was from the beginning to the end that
    without God
There is no way to save ourselves, no freedom,
    no providing
Against the time of trouble, no good feeling. Only one
Who made the universe and sees time in one glance
Deserves our songs, our praise.
    No nod, no blink, no dream
But God in the material jolts us, wakes us,
    gives us speech
That breaks our bondage, steadies wavers, sets us straight.

Praise only one. If our mouths held sounds like
    oceans water
And our tongues rippled standing waves, our lips
    stretched wide
As the horizon, our eyes both sun and moon, our hands
    spread
Wings like eagles on the updraft, our feet light,
It were not enough to thank you, praise you, say
    your name
Which can't be said, for all done for our fathers and for us.

You brought us out of Egypt and the house of bondage,
Fed us in famine, let us prosper amid plenty,
Saved us from the sword, the plague, from evil
    and disease.
As you have helped us until now, may you always
Keep us, God, upon the side of mercy.
And so we raise our arms, and dance, and sing, and speak
(Your gifts) inspired by the need to name,
Each mouth a thanks, each tongue an oath, each knee
Bent, thumping on the hollow earth as we remember
    the song that says:
"My bones cry out   'Public Defender
No tongue for hire, he   parries the spoilers'"
(Like what? same as who? how compares is to all?)
Along with the singer, I answer:
    "My soul remembers but does not
        know how to say the Name."

Powerful namelessness, doer of awe, most high,
    the ruler, the fullness where time comes from,
David has written:
    "Rejoice in the LORD, and be honest:
    For praise is a song from the upright."
In the mouth of the upright find praise;
In the words of the just hear your blessing;
The speech of believers exalts you;
In the middle of meaning, all's holy.

Wherever the children of Israel assemble
in every generation we remember, and we sing
    your songs of praise.
    For all that's made
is made your praise and we, remembering
our duty offer more than all the words and praises
sung by David, your anointed, Israel's sweet singer.

Praise God, heaven and earth, now and forever;
    we do, as did our fathers' fathers, offer fitting praise.

Bless you, LORD our God, cause for thanksgiving
    and master of wonders,
who hears songs and psalms, God, the life of the world.

All lift up their cups and say:

> Bless you, LORD our God, ruler of the universe,
>   who created the fruit of the vine.
>
> Barukh attah adonai eloheinu melech ha'olam
>   boré p'ri ha'gafen.
>
> בָּרוּךְ אַתָּה ה' אֱלֹהֵינוּ מֶלֶךְ הָעוֹלָם
> בּוֹרֵא פְּרִי הַגָּפֶן

Drink the fourth cup while reclining. Recite the final blessing.

Bless you, LORD our God, ruler of the universe,
    for the vine and its fruit, for the fields' harvest,
and bless you for the wide and pleasant land
    you gave our fathers and to us,
to eat the fruit, and be fulfilled, and know good.

O God, remember Israel your chosen people,
  and Jerusalem, your city,
Mount Zion, where your name lives, your altar
  and your home,
and build Jerusalem your holy city quickly, in our day
  and bring us there, together, to enjoy it.
We will bless you for it.
Let us rejoice on this Festival of Unleavened Bread
  for God is good and blesses all.
Thank you for the land, and for the fruit of the vine.

Bless you, LORD our God,
  for the land and for the fruit of the vine.

Barukh attah adonai al ha'aretz v'al p'ri ha'gafen.

בָּרוּךְ אַתָּה ה' עַל הָאָרֶץ וְעַל פְּרִי הַגָּפֶן

NIRTZAH/ נִרְצָה

The Passover Seder is done according to law and custom.
As we have lived to celebrate it here
  so may we celebrate it in the years to come.
O pure and higher than our thought,
  return the children, Israel, your love.
Lead your people quickly up to Zion, singing.

Next year in Jerusalem!

L'shana ha'baa bi'rushalayim ha'benuya!

לְשָׁנָה הַבָּאָה בִּירוּשָׁלַיִם הַבְּנוּיָה

THE HYMNS

After the Seder Service, some or all of these songs can be recited or sung by the celebrants. With luck, someone knows the tunes, and maybe can carry a tune. The lyrics are old folk songs for children, in the same form as the nursery rhyme, "The House that Jack Built."

AND IT CAME TO PASS, AT MIDNIGHT

You made miracles, at night
When watchers blink to see through night.
Abraham conquered four kings by night,
 And it came to pass, at midnight
You blighted Gerar in a dream by night,
You warned Laban on the night
Before. Israel wrestled with an angel all night.
 And it came to pass, at midnight
You crushed Egypt's first-born seed. The night-
Mare of a loaf of bread doomed Midian one night.
You cut down Sisera's armies under starry night.
 And it came to pass, at midnight
You turned the taunter's army into a corpses' camp.
  Overnight
The dragon Bel fell from his pedestal, while in the night
Daniel dreamed mysteries of coming night.
 And it came to pass, at midnight
Belshazzar perished in God's cups that night.
Daniel, reader of the words, stayed with lions for a night.
Haman the hater wrote his letters late at night.
 And it came to pass, at midnight
You toppled Haman during Ahasuerus' sleepless night.
You tread the winepress; asked, "What of the night?"
You answer, "The day cometh, and also the night,"
 And it came to pass, at midnight
Bring quickly, LORD, the day which is not day or night.
The day is yours, God, and so is the night.
Set guards about your city day and night,
Give us vision clear by day by night,
 And it came to pass, at midnight

ADIR HU

God is strong, God will build the Temple soon:
Quickly, while we're living, soon,
Build the Temple soon.

God alone, stark and strong,
        God will build the Temple soon:
Quickly, while we're living, soon,
Build the Temple soon.

God of light, out of time,
        God will build the Temple soon:
Quickly, while we're living, soon,
Build the Temple soon.

God's own grace on this place,
        God will build the Temple soon:
Quickly, while we're living, soon,
Build the Temple soon.

God, the wisdom and the legend,
        God will build the Temple soon:
Quickly, while we're living, soon,
Build the Temple soon.

God who made the universe,
        God will build the Temple soon:
Quickly, while we're living, soon,
Build the Temple soon.

God makes meaning, law, redemption,
        God will build the Temple soon:
Quickly, while we're living, soon,
Build the Temple soon.

God keep us on the side of mercy,
        God will build the Temple soon:
Quickly, while we're living, soon,
Build the Temple soon.

WHO KNOWS ONE?

Who knows one?
I know one:
One is God of heaven and earth.

Who knows two?
I know two.
Two stone tablets of the Law;
One is God of heaven and earth.

Who knows three?
I know three:
Three believing Patriarchs;
Two stone tablets of the Law;
One is God of heaven and earth.

Who knows four?
I know four:
Four fruitful Matriarchs;
Three believing Patriarchs;
Two stone tablets of the Law;
One is God of heaven and earth.

Who knows five?
I know five:
Five the Books of Moses;
Four fruitful Matriarchs;
Three believing Patriarchs;
Two stone tablets of the Law;
One is God of heaven and earth.

Who knows six?
I know six:
Six sections of Mishnah;
Five the Books of Moses;
Four fruitful Matriarchs;
Three believing Patriarchs;
Two stone tablets of the Law;
One is God of heaven and earth.

Who knows seven?
I know seven:
Seven days of the week;
Six sections of Mishnah;
Five the Books of Moses;
Four fruitful Matriarchs;
Three believing Patriarchs;
Two stone tablets of the Law;
One is God of heaven and earth.

Who knows eight?
I know eight:
Eight days before the foreskin's cut;
Seven days of the week;
Six sections of Mishnah;
Five the Books of Moses;
Four fruitful Matriarchs;
Three believing Patriarchs;
Two stone tablets of the Law;
One is God of heaven and earth.

Who knows nine?
I know nine:
Nine months to make a human child;
Eight days before the foreskin's cut;
Seven days of the week;
Six sections of Mishnah;
Five the Books of Moses;
Four fruitful Matriarchs;
Three believing Patriarchs;
Two stone tablets of the Law;
One is God of heaven and earth.

Who knows ten?
I know ten:
Ten, the Ten Commandments;
Nine months to make a human child;
Eight days before the foreskin's cut;
Seven days of the week;
Six sections of Mishnah;

Five the Books of Moses;
Four fruitful Matriarchs;
Three believing Patriarchs;
Two stone tablets of the Law;
One is God of heaven and earth.

Who knows eleven?
I know eleven:
Eleven stars in Joseph's dream;
Ten, the Ten Commandments;
Nine months to make a human child;
Eight days before the foreskin's cut;
Seven days of the week;
Six sections of Mishnah;
Five the Books of Moses;
Four fruitful Matriarchs;
Three believing Patriarchs;
Two stone tablets of the Law;
One is God of heaven and earth.

Who knows twelve?
I know twelve:
Twelve tribes of Israel;
Eleven stars in Joseph's dream;
Ten, the Ten Commandments;
Nine months to make a human child;
Eight days before the foreskin's cut;
Seven days of the week;
Six sections of Mishnah;
Five the Books of Moses;
Four fruitful Matriarchs;
Three believing Patriarchs;
Two stone tablets of the Law;
One is God of heaven and earth.

Who knows thirteen?
I know thirteen:
Thirteen attributes of God;
Twelve tribes of Israel;
Eleven stars in Joseph's dream;

Ten, the Ten Commandments;
Nine months to make a human child;
Eight days before the foreskin's cut;
Seven days of the week;
Six sections of Mishnah;
Five the Books of Moses;
Four fruitful Matriarchs;
Three believing Patriarchs;
Two stone tablets of the Law;
One is God of heaven and earth.

HAD GADYA

One kid,
      One little kid
My father bought for two zuzim.

A cat passed by and ate the kid,
      One little kid
My father bought for two zuzim.

A dog arrived and bit the cat that ate the kid,
      One little kid
My father bought for two zuzim.

A heavy stick then beat the dog that bit the cat
      That ate the kid,
      One little kid
My father bought for two zuzim.

A fire burned the heavy stick that beat the dog
            that bit the cat
That ate the kid,
      One little kid
My father bought for two zuzim.

Water put the fire out that burned the stick
            that beat the dog that bit the cat

That ate the kid,
     One little kid
My father bought for two zuzim.

An ox drank all that water up that doused the fire
          that burned the stick that beat the dog
          that bit the cat
That ate the kid,
     One little kid
My father bought for two zuzim.

A butcher slaughtered the ox that drank the water
          that doused the fire that burned the stick
          that beat the dog that bit the cat
That ate the kid,
     One little kid
My father bought for two zuzim.

The Angel of Death took off butcher who
          slaughtered the ox that drank the water
          that doused the fire that burned the stick
          that beat the dog that bit the cat
That ate the kid,
     One little kid
My father bought for two zuzim.

The Holy One then killed the Angel of Death
          who took off the butcher who slaughtered the ox
          that drank the water that doused the fire
          that burned the stick
          that beat the dog that bit the cat
That ate the kid,
     One little kid
My father bought for two zuzim.

www.ingramcontent.com/pod-product-compliance
Lightning Source LLC
Chambersburg PA
CBHW021147020426
42331CB00005B/936